THE
EXTREMELY UNOFFICIAL
AND
HIGHLY UNAUTHORIZED
STAR WARS KAMA SUTRA

by

S.N. Herder

ISBN-10: 1519483058
ISBN-13: 978-1519483058

THANKS

First and foremost, I would like to thank George Lucas. Without the amazing universe that he created, none of these silly little jokes would be possible. Sure, I might poke a little fun, but it is with good hearted intentions and a great love for Star Wars and everything it has made possible. I'd also like to thank my friends, family, and girlfriend who put up with an unending barrage of dirty toy pics and sexual references in their inboxes and texts. There are some things they've seen that cannot be unseen.

TABLE OF CONTENTS

ABOUT THE AUTHOR

SN Herder has a little too much time on his hands. While others are out curing cancer and coming up with brilliant alternative power sources, he spends his nights playing with toys and sending sophomoric pictures to his friends. Amazingly, SN Herder is not single, but what is even more amazing is that his girlfriend actually thinks he's funny.

INTRODUCTION

This book was created for Star Wars fans with a slightly twisted sense of humor. It is a parody of the characters in the Star Wars universe and created with all the love in the world that I've got for them (yes, even Jar Jar). Within these pages, you'll find all your favorite Star Wars characters, represented by the action figures that I have purchased over the years, engaged in all manner of absurd sexual positions and situations. Don't try any of the positions in this book. Most of them are not physically achievable, and I've got no idea where you'd be able to find a Rancor, anyway. Don't buy this book for small children. That's just stupid. Buy it for your boyfriend, girlfriend, husband, wife, friend or parent. Buy it for anyone you know who loves Star Wars and knows that the internal temperature of a Taun Taun is always going to be "Luke Warm."

May the Force be with you.

THE FORCE AWAKENS

Starring

Luke Skywalker

ATTACK OF THE CLONES

Starring

The Clone Troopers

IT'S A CRAP!

Starring

Admiral Ackbar and Wookiee Warrior

THE APPRENTICE

Starring

Emperor Palpatine and Darth Maul

BIGGER...

AND SMELLIER ON THE INSIDE!

Starring

Luke Skywalker, Taun Taun, Dalek, TARDIS,
Cyberman and the 8th and 11th Doctors

EMBRACE THE DARK SIDE

Starring

Yoda, Yaddle, Luke Vader and R2-D2

OOTINI

Starring

The Jawas

LET THE WOOKIEE WIN

Starring

Chewbacca, R2-D2 and C-3PO

IT'S A TRAP!

Starring

Admiral Ackbar and Ahsoka Tano

THE TRENCH RUN

Starring

The Death Star

AT-AT STYLE

Starring

AT-AT #1, AT-AT #2, Han Solo and R2-D2

THE MASTER VADER

Starring

Darth Vader

YUB YUB YUB
THREE EWOKS IN A TUB

Starring

Wicket the Ewok, Romba and Graak

THE PERFECT MAN

Starring

Princess Leia Organa and Han Solo (in Carbonite)

THE DROIDS I'M LOOKING FOR!

Starring

Clone Trooper Rys, R2-D2 and C-3PO

COO SA DOE SHAG ATEEMA, SCHUTTA?

(Who is the slave now, bitch?)

Starring

Jabba the Hutt, Princess Leia Organa,
Han Solo (in Carbonite) and Salacious B. Crumb

REVENGE OF THE SITH FIST

Starring

Mace Windu and Emperor Palpatine

THE OEDIPUS

Starring

Luke Skywalker, Padme Amidala and Darth Vader

LUKE WARM

Starring

Luke Skywalker and The Taun Taun

THE XXX WING

Starring

Jorg Sacul (George Lucas), Jek Porkins, Biggs Darklighter, Dak Ralter, Tiree and Davish Krail

THE BACTA TANK

(AKA: 2 in the tank, 1 in the stank)

Starring

Luke Skywalker and Aayla Secura

STAR WARS KAMA SUTRA

51

BOBA FETTISH

Starring

Boba Fett, Pulp Fiction's The Gimp and Salacious B. Crumb

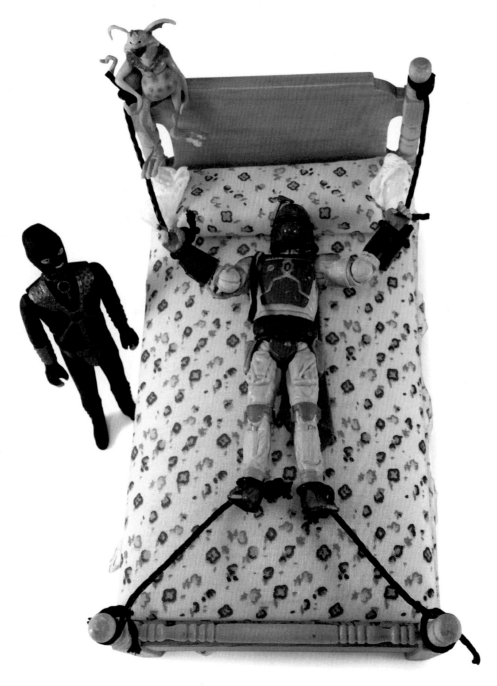

THE SLAVE LAY-ER

Starring

Jabba the Hutt, Princess Leia Organa and Salacious B. Crumb

HENSON'S CREATURE SHOP

Starring

Jabba the Hutt, Darth Maul and Princess Leia Organa

ROCK, PAPER, XIZOR, LIZARD, SPOCK

Starring

Geodude the Pokemon, Prince Xizor, Mr. Spock
and one lucky dinosaur

A DISTURBANCE IN THE FORCE

Starring

Luke Skywalker, Padme Amidala, Oola,
C-3PO, Yarna D'al Gargan and Yaddle

THE HOLIDAY SPECIAL

Starring

Bea Arthur and Lumpy

CENSORED

This position was so bad that we've decided to pretend it never happened and to never release it in any format... even though it featured Bea Arthur doing unspeakable things to Lumpy.

HAN SHOT FIRST

Starring

Princess Leia Organa, Han Solo and Greedo

SIZE MATTERS NOT

Starring

Yoda and Rancor

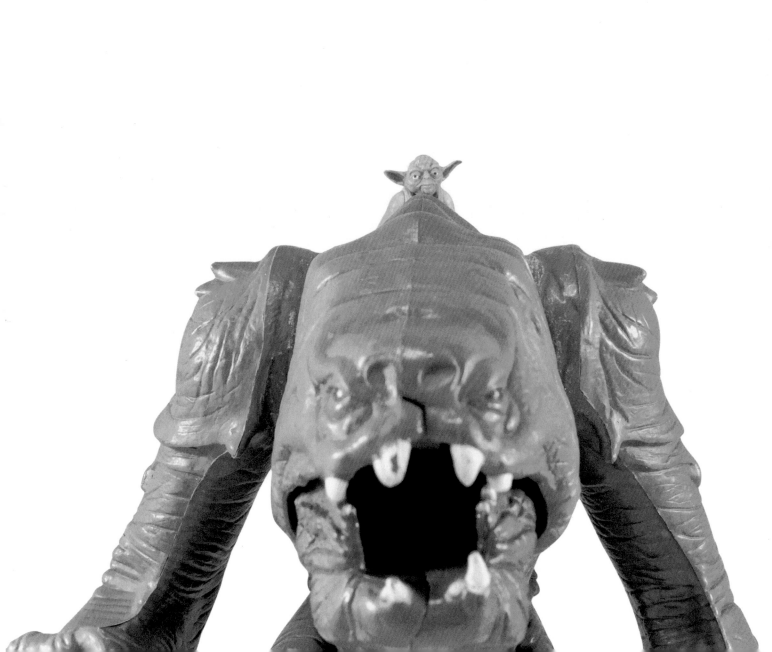

THAT'S NO MOON!

Starring

Luke Skywalker, Obi-Wan Kenobi and Yarna D'al Gargan

REVENGE FOR THE PREQUELS:
STAR WARS STRIKES BACK

Starring

Jorg Sacul (George Lucas), Darth Vader, Yoda, Obi-Wan Kenobi, Admiral Ackbar, Han Solo, Wicket The Ewok, Emperor Palpatine, Lando Calrissian Chewbacca, R2-D2, C-3PO, Luke Skywalker, Jawa, and Taun Taun

THE SPEEDER BIKE

Starring

Wicket the Ewok and Scout Trooper

THE SHARPSHOOTERS

Starring

Aurra Sing, Storm Trooper, Snow Trooper,
Clone Trooper and Scout Trooper

THE RIDE-ALONG

Starring

Dewback, Ronto and The Jawas

FEEL THE POWER OF THE FORCE

Starring

Yoda, Luke Skywalker and R2-D2

THE HAND SOLO

Starring

Han Solo, Princess Leia Organa and Boba Fett

TWO GIRLS, ONE CUP...
OF BANTHA MILK

Starring

Aayla Secura, Aunt Beru and Service Droid

WORKS EVERY TIME

Starring

Lando Calrissian, Princess Leia Organa, Aurra Sing and Oola

DO, OR DO NOT…

Starring

Yoda, Yarna D'al Gargan, Oola and Aurra Sing

CANTINA UGLY

Starring

Obi-Wan Kenobi, Luke Skywalker, Chewbacca,
Han Solo, Greedo, Ponda Baba, Dr. Evazan,
Yarna D'al Gargan, Aurra Sing, Oola, Yaddle,
Jabba The Hutt's Dancers (Greeata, Rystáll, and Lyn Me)

FEEDING TIME

Starring

Yarna D'al Gargan and The Pigs from "Pass the Pigs"

I KNOW...

Starring

Han Solo and Princess Leia Organa

THE FIRST ORDER

Starring

Jar Jar Binks, Kylo Ren and First Order Trooper

Cinnamon bun hair
A shiny gold bikini
Let me see your Boushh

Leia's dejected
For what once was erected
So sad, Han shot first

No more hand solo
Vader's saber stole his joy
Luke was a righty

There is another.
Wish Yoda had said something
Before I kissed my sister

A lonely Hoth night
Only Taun Tauns are in sight
They smell worse inside

By my size you judge?
It isn't the saber's length
But the force unleashed

Vader's first force choke
Didn't expect to love it
Welcome to the dark side Ani

Yarna D'al Gargan
Six-breasted palace dancer
Jabba's special gal

Midichlorians
Bad ideas threaten fan hopes
Jar Jar Binks must die

Boba Fett engulfed
Swallowed ever so deeply
Within a Sarlaac pit

INDEX

Made in the USA
Middletown, DE
02 December 2016